I0884877

salmonpoetry

Publishing Irish & International
Poetry Since 1981

ALSO BY JAMES RAGAN

POETRY

In the Talking Hours
Womb-Weary
The Hunger Wall
Lusions
Selected: The Tallinn Poems
Too Long a Solitude
The World Shouldering I
To Sing Us Out of Silence
The Chanter's Reed

PLAYS

Saints
The Landlord
Commedia

TRANSLATIONS

Yevgeny Yevtushenko:
The Collected Poems, 1952-1990
(ed./trans. with Albert C. Todd)
Henry Holt Publishers

ESSAYS

Poet as Prophet: Anthology of Magazine Verse, Monitor Books, 1988
A Renaissance in Chinese Literature, Los Angeles Times, 1988
Language and the You Know Generation, Delaware University Press, 1989
The Artist in the Era of Intellectual Recession, East Wind Publishers, 1996
The Oscars Through a Lens Darkly, Variety Magazine Publications, 1998

The Chanter's Reed

JAMES RAGAN

This collection is published in 2020 by
Salmon Poetry, Cliffs of Moher, County Clare, Ireland
www.salmonpoetry.com email: info@salmonpoetry.com

ISBN 978-1-912561-88-9

Cover & Title Page Photography: *Jessie Lendennie*
Cover Design & Typesetting: *Siobhán Hutson*
Printed in Ireland by Sprint Print

For John and Theresa Ragan

who taught me that art
is the gift of truth
and passion

Contents

III

Primal

IV

Astonishment

The Chanter's Reed

The Bells on the Tabla Fields

I have waited well beyond the bells
for the slunking cart to rime its rims
along the mud-ruts, snaking a path
into the road. I lie near a stream,
my head low between the stalks,
the wheat splashed against the sky
in golden splinters. Leaning high
into a cloud, a fox sings its sermon
to a night owl, a sleep flower rakes
the air with soft aromas. A sparrow
drifts up across the birch, no longer
fixed to the longitude of sound.
The oak, reaching out its leafy brush,
leans to print its signature on a full moon.
I have lain here far too long,
believing that the past will settle,
find its mate in nostalgia
or the gift of an un-thought future.
What needs to be done and undone
bears repeating like a desert
warring blood out of sand.
All that is present eludes me.
I am no longer dreamed by the wolf
who howls to lose his memory of me.
by the crow, ravening the sunset,
its black wings in flight, shadowing
the hieroglyphics of a charred forest.
I am no longer lulled by the moon
painting the sky in hues of red and yellow
to rid me from its sight. I lie here only
to be found, a spent and sodden soul,
deaf to the mystery of bells
sainting out their haunt of poems,
waiting for the infant birth of an inspiration
to flaunt its creation at the very moment
the crow's wing glides to eclipse the sun.

I.

Afterplay

The voice of the intellect is a soft one,
but does not rest until it has gained a hearing.

SIGMUND FREUD

The Chanter's Reed

The astonishing sound I hear when a birch clicks into beats
or the way a bench shifts, on sitting, wrenching out its bolts;

the breath a trashcan mouths through its lip-sync of metal
swinging into jagged rhythms, or the wheeze a balloon exhales

to announce its flight to freedom—these are the roiled
notes of dissonance he scores, conducting his bagpipe

through the bellow's push and bob of air, past the Babel
symphony of pipes, two as stunted twins, the third a longer port

over-lording both, and the spigot spouting out a language
dogs have mimed into pitched whimpers. Hear his finger

torqueing on the windpipe, the pouch that nestles snugly at the elbow,
the strength of blow that fills the chanter's reed with passion,

breeding the wind-drip of drones into the undertone
like an open freezer buzzing or a breeze whistling in the fountain sluice.

There is no sound as benevolent as the after-play he holds
in his lungs' long breath, no art refined as the scrum of notes

skirling high above the alder, no sight as reverent
as the shock of nuance the blind child hears, stump-still, amazed.

Her wheelchair detours to the piper's sired tune, a wallet opens. She spills
a coin into his pauper's sack, a doting patronage to save his soul,

and turning to salute, she hums a requiem, one ear tuned to the mind's
dance with the heart, the other, to art's lingering after-play.

Blinded by My Senses

You've asked me to write completely with the senses
and imagine that a stranger is blind. So I think of a willow,
cut off at the thigh, a stump, inverted, roots to the ground.
The space of air above, that he is leaning into,
shoves him tumbling into dust. A strand of fog
rises where the slug of his bark has shrunk the sky.
The air, he says, tastes like the dried skin of a grape,
the ground like lumber sod, years in a damp cellar.
I believe it's me who's losing sight, and all I see is size
as if his head like the shrinking ball of the sun
were being sucked dry by the planet-spin of my eyes.
                                        Perhaps, he's only a fallen limb
with spurs growing out to prick him up to speed.
I refuse to hear the hint of his sobbing. His glasses
frost in the mud-puddle where he lies
like a wet newspaper, the print bleeding.
He smells like a dried peach rotted by dew,
like parched hair, hours in the sun after rain.
I imagine his shoulders thrust back like a bull,
anxious for the sword. He swings his tongue
back and forth as if to lick the wounds from his eyes.
                                        I refuse the sound of his pleading,
the longing to be lifted, brushed off, and on his way.
I've heard this plea before, always when I'm dreaming
about the drunken neighbor, who chopped down
the rope and willow, and his daughter's past. Wait,
this is not about the stranger. Perhaps, my neighbor
is imagining me, blind, my arms stretched thin
from squeezing out some small privilege of lost emotion
into a scream. I should carry a log to show him
how strong I am, that I can lift him if I dared, if I chose
to hold the fallen limb he hunts for his repentance.
He's worn out his mind with the belief that I will.
I sense the sound of my own sobbing.
I can't believe my eyes. It's as though I had to hear
something twice to see something, blind.

for Robert Bly

On Lines I'm Not Sure Are My Own

You tell me violins have no sound,
that you come only to play
at night when notes are silent,
and I am breathing sleep
into my own small seeds of talk,
the lost words of the day's memory.

I worry you up too easily
each time I speak, the tongue
bowing the litter of teeth
into quarrels of a sort.
You tell me I am playing
the lost words of my youth,
each squeal, the string's
syllable of pain.

You tell me I am naked
in your eyes when the strings
go soft at the moment
of our whispering.
I can barely hear the breath
of no sound, but the words,
they worry me. They are pretending
to speak. The violins warn me of this.

Rage

All day, I've waited for breath to climb onto the tongue,
not easily, some might say with a gasping stutter,
sliding down the throat's ribbed spine
to find the word that refuses to be spoken, its silence
wrapped like shade in the lung's bowl of darkness.
What could I know of nuance, its shape or sound,
elusive like the scent of saffron, neither giving nor forgiving,
how in moments of light, when wilder has gardened its heart,
it fades with the dying roots of regret? I would sooner reach out
to a crow's beak or climb a steeple and believe as many do
in the height and point of things, how in merciful times
a syllable's utterance of guilt might suffice. All day I've wondered
what in time is too long a time to kneel before a flowered grave
until a death is honored. What in time is too silent a word to ban
the triggered power that breeds contempt for a generation's grief.
For weeks I've wandered, searching the riddle of letters
for any assemblage of sounds I could justify for an instance
of repentance, for any gift of redemption I could set free
from the depth of world-pity. In a word, *enough*
is not word enough to silence the rage sorrowed in this song.

for the Young Innocents Lost to Us in Mass Shootings

Remembering My Lai After Leaving the VA Hospital Healing Farm

22 Veterans Commit Suicide Per Day.
(AP March, 16, 2017)

a

All morning the claw of darkness
carves its shadows on the logs.
I lie awake to crackling fire
or what I think are leaves,
the day's bonding of the wind and frost,
nesting between the rafter's crotch.
I stare past suspended eaves,
the corners of the walls, the screams
that splash across the floor,
seeking hands to touch,
past the window's warp
to where the village ditch bodies-up
its grave of buried limbs,
and starved wood rats
smear their leather lips
across the tongues of shoes,
at you, drowned once again
where sleep begins.

b

Outside, gun-flashes,
gauzed in a muzzling fog of orange,
are shuttered by the latticed shadow
playing possum cool among the trees.
It swings on branches across the TV's mirror.
It scrapes shattered faces
from keeled bamboo nets,
from the tope and hooch,

from the river's bed and shapes reflections
like fingerprints along your face.
I chase the mewling haunt of flares,
shells of lightning at my heels,
along retreating fire light,
the cobbling of mortar rounds,
the sounds of children
bellying deep into the black nightshade,
into the blue flame of the lotus
where their faces root,
flower and are forgotten.

c

I walk out of memory, out of a God's hate,
into their mercy,
shapeless like the guilt of peace
we share in sleep's conjuration
where seasons never change
and shadows are consumed
by a burning patch of sunlight,
loitering between the trees
like a starved bear
protecting its own.

for those who stood up to the massacre:
Army Pilot Hugh Thomson Jr, Specialist
Lawrence Colburn, Crew Chief Glenn Andreotta
Viet Nam, March 16, 1968

Under the Sign of the Societe D'Encouragement Pour Industrie Nationale.

a

Now the tenth band jams in the rain off *Les Deux Magots.*
The *Montmartre* bus has stalled to let the trombones pass.
A gendarme sips a demitasse to a flutist playing Sati,
and a bassoon sows a note in the Flora canopy.
All of Paris is encouraged on the feast of *Magdeleine* to bury all spite.
Art will not apologize to the *adversaires* of possibility.
Fear is no willing servant to the language of languor or to memory's
terror at Saint-Denis. Now the moon rains its shadows
through the Rose window scrim of Notre Dame.
The night will hang its lanterns to the stars for Charlie Hebdo
on *Le Jour de la Musique*. Even now, a kettle-drum
beats its sticks to marching measure.
Music, like a nursing marm, gives its peace of mind
to the healing war-wounded, the hopping one-leggers
who cluck like drummers dancing their wood.

b

According to the Law of Henry IV, Paris was to be created in a day
and with it light. No shade should be allowed to measure up
to the height of a royal oak, nor building scale the sky higher
than the eyes can see or the width of the street.
No one by law could be denied the sun's lay at his feet.
Doors when they open should ride to one's reach,
heavening out in showered reflections to the terrace above,
and windows, wide as the mat straddling a dormer sill,
might let the rays vault up to the ceilings.
Curtains should not lace the glass in filigree,
and should a cloud be rude enough to linger for a storm
the dark has gathered up to stir the day's terror in night's debris,
chandeliers should sway to chime their leaves forever
as if to allow each prism's beam a universe of fire
to flame the street lamps from *Notre Dame* to the *Tuilleries.*

dedicated to all Parisiennes, April 15, 2019

Rumination

Imprecision is an affront to truth.

The snow has no thoughts to rime,
the wind no guilt to grieve. The stone
has no laughter in its veins, the rain
no pity for its harsh thumb-tick on a tin roof
until a word is written, syllabled not in joy
or grief, but in the passion of reflection,
restoring conviction to an emotion that's died.
The *word* wants to believe it feels or thinks
and can achieve heights of understanding
through a phrase that's spoken, a short phrase
or a phrase, long and kicking
like the sudden stutter of an eye or a voice
that shouts on finding the precise word,
the word that has no other place to be
but in the space at hand, this space, right here,
alone, chanting in a forest of meanings
from the lost forgotten branch it was fated to climb.

Sometimes a Fly

flies away backward
as I do with any dandling swipe
                    or wind-whistle
of a hand's swift
sweep across the eye.
                    More than once
I've skidded
through my mind
                    backward
into an insight I couldn't stand,
instant as a slap
          across a prurient thought,
or withdrawn
when instinct blurs
                    what is real
or what is simply
the natural course of things
                              like hate.
A fly flies away backward
because it is chaste,
                    unnerved
by intrusion,
confident in flight,
                    a surly buzzing
jag of a laugh
each time I swing through
                    its flurried dip and stall.
It mocks me now
as the penitent I am,
                    when missing
the butt of its head
with the tenth swat
                    I invest,
occupied with speed
and not with judging
                    the inch of path

its tenored voice will take
or the misdirection
                                        it will calculate
to succeed,
while I, too often,
                                          fail
by trusting fate's
cocked rush to blind choice.

Two Opossums Lying at a Train Crossing

They were exhausted, tired of the art
of feigning sleep, and worse, of giving death
a certain cuteness to its slumber.
This was their pact, not to see who would leap
first off the track before the train's light skewered the rail
to learn they were not trundled branches
fallen from an overhang of birch or, at the least,
a patch of sod dribbled from a rumbling cart.
No, they were couriers of imminent change
to the sleeping travelers, unaware of the coming
swift shock of the caulking cork to their bottled lives,
each in their pillowed way, pretending
not to notice by the berth's sudden shift
that their place in the universe was about to end
with skidding speed into lasting blindness;
not knowing that the two furriers of doom
had committed, solemnly, to playing
their final role as drunken souls, sprawled
across the path of comic chance and tragic fate.
Theirs was a travesty of sorts, each assured
that one would wake the other
in the event they had over-staged the scene.
After all, they had nothing to lose but sleep,
and having learned their parts well, were at peace
with knowing they had dutifully studied
the eyes of all those who, for years, had studied them
like adoring acolytes at the feet of masters,
and who, in an instant of time, had learned nothing
in the tyranny of silence, as alluring and deadly
as apathy and *ennui* in quiet repose.

The Dumbing Down Finale

to the Body Politic, Nov. 8, 2016

There must have been at one time a knot
that formed in our skulls, that loosed itself
and crossed like a scout's tie, full of honor and brass.
There must have been a slowing down of thought,
the mind's seduction we failed to suspect, a bullyboy
with the quotidian play of cartoon teeth
squawking like a waxwing or a yak that talks.
Charisma is too often a price to pay for a mind's death.
It's the prancing bulge of a braggart breast
or the tower-minded ego, that occults itself
to power and denies us choice.
Lead us poor souls to fear the facile, the irrational
honed sparring of tongues in a sot's spin
of a boorish rant, or the hate that grows like nails
in a Klansman's thought. Teach us to loathe
the worship of a culture's tabloid spell.
Spare us the terror of a lie's dominion,
how the fig-wasp germinates on a host tree
in the swallowing scales of a Banyan leaf.
Teach us to resist the science of denial, our mouth-
sore love for delusion, haunting the mind, dumbing us
to the catbird tweets of the bullyboy's scorn.
Save us from the demagogue's sentient charm,
how it intoxicates the baiting of our fears,
pretends us to greatness, rallies us to shame.
Show us mercy for the loving birth of our kind.

Submission

... normalizing deviance downward.

Senator Daniel Patrick Moynihan

I can hardly sleep these days, propped up
like a lean-to in order that my mind won't crick
into a posture of submission
or that my eyes won't squint into flatline hyphens,
linking sight to image in a world
that cheats its reflection into being what it denies.
I want to believe that a bullet can fail its purpose
and refuse to serve the fired trigger that sustains its being.
I want to believe that no finesse of paltering logic
can shift the weight of language into a dandering
dance of raptured equivocation. I would rather
believe in a child's innocence of dreaming gnomes
than float my trust on a stream of delusional rants.
You might believe my future is behind me,
and I'm looking forward to the past.

Even now I barely see the flash of light
from the window type its phrase across the page.
It would have me believe in inspiration,
how in this cyber land of mirrors that smoke,
thoughts that rot, an insight like a rattling roof,
that shingles out its years in sunlight and rainfall,
can only doom itself to crack.
I won't be swayed to the way of cynics,
the praying skeptics and skull-bone preachers
who sleep too long in the faith of mirroring
all the faultless faces they construct or have become
in their broken universe of loss.

You might say I speak too much and say too little.
Even now I pretend to laughter in this *tele-evasion* of talk.
Show me a rime of consonants and vowels
where a single image can rise above a prayer's cant
in sound and flight to breach the limits
of a false beyond. Show me how in conscience
I can ignore the spit of a bigot's spite
bursting at will like a tongue's nimbus shooting out
a thousand rumors out of a lone innuendo.
I will not be pulled down to rub my mind
like a tired eye or a funny-bone that stings,
then tingles into nothing that laughs.

I won't be pulled down to words of worry
with the hope, in time, they'll shout or sing
until a fact can outlive a doubt that outlives a lie,
and a word can break the boundaries of its will
and learn to soar. Show me all the truths I've whored
to fell the taunting tyranny of a deviant mind,
and I will show you hope and dread,
one in exit, the other at the door.
Perhaps, you're not getting what I mean to mean.
You might believe my words have lost their dreaming.
Perhaps, I'm not being clear. Perhaps,
you're only hearing what I sing.

After All

After all, you say, even the leaves are falling.
Your smile, scarred by the pain that brings you here
smiles back. A master of delay, you stall time
to score the chart, to sweat the scalpel
through to its ribs. Today, you tune your cough
politely. Your hand, a tunnel to the heart,
collapses in mine to soothe the shock.
There are nights, you say, the ice cools slowly
like stale jokes or linen days you bleed for
to win a meal. You pretend well, a mind-reader,
buzzing twice to leave the room, remembering
the lark you hear, trapped behind the bed screen
out in the snow. We listen, your talk pressed
against my ear, stethoscopic, trained to hear
bones knock, to a flutter of wings, something
in the odor of your breath, dying to be let out.

***

All day, you speak of release, how to free
the bond between flesh and spirit, how they close
in as one, each to the other, promising
at the very moment when night pre-empts the day,
a profound light will inspire the miraculous
shock of a mortal comeback, as if death were simply
a day of cancellation, a day of begging out
from the daily task of breathing, *s'il vu plait*—
a day of learning back the trust, that even truth
has warts and wants to hide itself from those
who confuse it with beauty. Truth, you say,
is beauty only to those who believe all
that lies within the sheen of words, is polished
to hide the doubt beneath. You laugh through
doubts that some still think to be astonishingly true,
as in the need for gods to be imagined,
or that time stops once the watch has broken.
After all, you say, consciousness can prove to be
a brittle thing, but conscience should never be.

***

Now, the lark that visited in June, and again
during the cedar's rust in autumn, has returned.
You insist that at tonight's final breath,
we should practice the moan of silence, the hum
of fearing the worst at the moment of dread,
while laughing to know it's moved on.
In your leaving, you insist on laughter,
that you're only going out to bend the roadway
to an oval, so that you can walk it backwards
and end, looking forward to the past. You insist,
with shortened breath, it's sometimes best
to take the long way round to find the shortest
way home. After all, you say, it's not how long
you walk it, but how amazed you are at being lost
in each found inspiration, that truly matters.

for my brother

The Gift

Once you feel that memory is loving you less,
that dreams inebriate your saddest thoughts
like sighs with no particular meaning,
visit the one thought you've forgotten to recall,
the one that breathes like a lapping dog
heeling for food, the one with the look
of a soiled rag you've forgotten to wash.
You've hungered it long enough,
for such a small fear as believing
it will not feed you in return.
You want too much out of gifting
as if giving desires a just reward or a yield
like counter change or a seed
you've watered into bloom. It may be,
you're starving for affection, always needing
to rake in attention with the last word
of a conversation to be your own.
Find the one thought you're dying to recall,
the one you've been storing in memory
like a blanket saved for a child's birth.
That's it — your embrace wrapping life
as an offering to the world. This is your gift,
not the wanting but the giving,
not the infant eyes out of the womb
opening to light, but the yield—
the one thought an infant saves
to remember is the first touch of your hand
as the greatest want to be born.

II.

Imagine

The lunatic, the lover, and the poet
are of imagination all compact.

WILLIAM SHAKESPEARE

Cradled

It could be said, I was born of balky stock. I could not be kept
from breathing the sweet scent of mulch and ferns in the furrowed scrub

of my mother's palm. I could not be lulled into believing that hell
might find redemption in the perpetual moan of prayer, or that Easter ash

she signed like a third eye to my brow was the signature of a forgiving hand.
Up from the mill where my brothers walked the bread queues,

and jazz-wagging tongues danced to the furnace heat of Fatha' Hines,
my father taught me not to settle into the reap of greed,

needled in the creweled stitching of the world's soul.
Happy just to sing, he fiddled a bow until his vision healed.

The steel, he said, condemns us to the open, what can we do against it,
Pittsburgh is an energy town. By the Nixon spring, I would not heel

my tongue or twist a pen into the cursing pain of subdued silence.
I would not concede to tie my feet like a wrestled lamb

or add my breath to the vengeful tribes of war. I refused to believe
that history must be forgiven. Condemned to intellect,

I learned to cock the quick fist of reason like the Reverend King
and go for the head where the thinking is, and not the arm that easily bends.

In my youth, I was slow to learn the art of forgiveness, as my mother could,
slow to share in the eyes' vision of compassion as my father had,

until I saw the earth's green swale of land cradled in space
by the fiddling bow of dark and light, appearing and reappearing

like a pumping heart through the glass of a camera eye,
blinking out from the cratered dust of a distant moon.

The Belly of a Spoon

When lacking inspiration, I'd sometimes imagine,
on the back of a spoon, the reflection of the soft
underbelly of a full moon, on which I'd lick my tongue
to taste the luminescence of light. I would lick
the spoon until the moon reflected the sun,
and my eyes could feed the fire in my words, starving
like splinters of flint that raged to be born.
And if the sun had dimmed its flame, I would lick
the bowl of the spoon for any residue of light
to feed my mind before despair released its rain
of darkness to claim my soul. I believed that victims
had in their minds an eternal view of their souls.
The infamous had no souls, having lost them
in memory to the brittle teeth of mind-demons to chew
and devour. The infamous would never lick a spoon.

Imagine Another

way of telling it, how it all comes to silence,
how, at first, you catch me unaware, hunched, hands on railings
of the lower Hudson, sulking in a huckster kind of stutter.
Sure, I'm quick to shade my eyes to light swelling
through the tunnel ducts, the kick of traffic gently shoving,
skidding through the slushing undertow of peppered snow.
You had even caught me dozing down among the drifters,
scraping plates like sweepers off the Bowery curbs,
watched me herding tourists into lines up to their eyes
in the neon glow of marquee lights, watched them root
in their broad way of standing. You hear me now
throttling my throat up from the underground,
leaning out to direct each cab passing in a flurry.
Some would marry my heart, were it not for the past
they've come to bury, dark as the eyes that haunt
their rear-view mirrors. I keep my dreaming close,
old as memory molding steel into girders scraping sky.
No one sees how swollen my eyes become, how I long
to lay back the day in a pigeon's park or *chic* café,
or prow the Ramble at the boating's cove with a symphony
at the Band Shell, roaring. If only I could be imagined
as I imagine myself, walking the long-cast shade
of the World One Tower to the avenues of Chelsea,
mending the minds of all the wounded, their thoughts
rising, like their will, from words half-broken.

Lament for a Milltown Son

As a boy wearing a man's heart,
I cuffed my sleeves as my father would.
The nuns said I was the boy whores searched for

when they joined the profession.
They said, boys become men,
thinking they look forward

to the nameplate dressing the desk,
the underclothes still straddled there
and the secretary. At night together in bed

I watch the same slavering dog
shag the couch and carpet. The photo of the children
reveals the centerfold of a young won wife.

When I lie down old in fantasy,
the nuns will say it's only the steelworker's son
lamenting his lack of progress.

When as a man in my dry month I roll
off the woman in the photo, the nuns will say
it is the wife bored with wearing a whore's heart.

No, I will reach for her breasts softly,
and fondly as my father said I would,
remembering the boy on the sleeve of her.

Drinking Ouzo at Kolonaki Square

I couldn't imagine this moment
should happen at all. The rain
has lit the scarf of lamp-light
you wear beneath the café's canopy.

A wind excites your hair
the way a painter not quite sure
of a final strand along the forehead
spars with air

nervously. Your glance meets
mine each time your lashes
tease the eyes, fluttering wild,
not for me, chairs away,
my roweled eye brushing its comb
along your cheek.

In Greece, it's said, when eyes meet,
a conversation ends. Only
the shell of a word remains
as I whisper low to romance your hair
like a bald man to fur on a coat.

I would rather not hear
the rasp of a tire skidding its pain
along the graveled curb
as I write *I need you*
on a note I pass to myself.
That will not be the poem.

God-proud woman with your lips
wet above the tongue's spur,
I want to speak
your language, to tell you
of the too full sky
and the child I wed to your body

or the words I will never speak or write
down, shy, un-translated
along your thighs.
If in memory we should meet,
you will see me staring, gratefully
at your face turning
backwards across the Square
to a shot of ouzo spilling, shattered,
a man slouching backward to a bus,
anonymous as sound
in the shard of breaking glass.

Not Every Girl Comes Naked to the Forest

just because I believe that fantasy is a right,
that ecstasy is my consolation for weaning off
        the grind of passion,
that somehow in the adolescence of the mind
        my imagination
has aged into a loose-fit coat I wear
        out of fear
that I'd be seen as less than one, a decimal,
        and of a sort who stammers
into words the lines of a Dylan rhyme, the kind
who waits because the moon has tricked me
        like a smile
into thinking I am the chosen, the winning
        ticket,
not because I conjured it up over lit wax and stone,
not because I willed it through the lottery
        of prayer
or because she shivers my eyes and arms
        into a sweat
that pretends its wash along my body,
or because it's night, and darkness wanes
        for light
to bathe the back-boughs of birch and cedar
        where I wait.
No, she will come to the forest for me this night
because the pines are naked and charred with absent limbs.
        She will come
because I've grown into the bark, a birthing branch
        for seeds to leaf in
while she awaits for me to green out into the munificence
of sunlight, into the sharing love of nurturing rain.

Stretching the Imagination

It's not enough to see the red or blue in paint to name its color
or coax a photograph to black and white out of shades of gray.
You must tease the mind, beyond all sense, and stretch the senses.
You must imagine the taste of shattered chips along a shred of elm,
blown dry from the wind's long day's dye of dust and rain.
You must drink the ruck of darkness to know the passion in light
that seeds the moon and dimming stars to ease the night's remorse.
I'm going out to iron the lawn today and tomorrow, and each day,
until I sap the sky's dark cloud from its cloth, until the stress,
that threads my mind's muscle to the bone, will cease its palling pain.
I might even create a bolt that's edible, that will screw the heart in
to keep from breaking, and the lungs as well, to keep each breathing
like a racer's engine revving up to test the tire's tread.
I might as well create a soul that's double-minded, one for dying
to drift beyond the map of breath, the other exciting a sprint
to incite its birth. I'm convinced that if I marry wit to imagination,
I can invent a thought to live in, stuck in the atrophy of infinite peace.
At this moment I'm thinking of chopping a waterfall into threads
so that I can swing from each strand like a spider monkey
until I've crossed the cratered trench to reach the shore's shallow end.
Consider the joy of mystery, how it hides just long enough
to be ignored, then returns in the imagination to amaze,
as if in a glorious moment of insight, I've just turned a rock over
and found the forgotten truths of a lost language.

On the Train to Cambridge, Through Ely

That's a joke, you see.
I'm full of jokes.

Imagine the man, talking, dim-witted,
who keeps waking up a conversation
he has carried on alone, carving his joke
into the air with a finger
he's been grooming, thumb and bone.

Across the aisle a scientist
speaks of *fibers* and *kinking*
and adds a corset to her thought,
the train in which we hardly matter
having passed through Ely on the dot.

We have traveled well beyond
her thesis, his finger moving closer
to the point. He says she's
full of it, the jokes, he means,
he's full of them, himself, and knows.

Again, she insists the world has kinked
beyond his peerage, while the joker ups
the ante with his tallest finger,
raising conversation to a science,
and the universe through man's good humor,
to nature's cruel joke.

Mugwampery

...to endeavor to put a respectable face on it.

I've watched the aging age, resigned
to the course of growing any crease in skin,
its browning galaxy of spokes
flamed out like a smoldering map
on the charred tree of the hand.
I've watched them limp into their borrowed knees,
cough their sneeze with choired spools of breath
as if rehearsing notes of spring or dispelling
a heard word that's off-put and off-color.
I've seen them fall into a chair
like shafts of walking lumber.
I've watched them breed at chessboards
like birchbarks wintering away until they bald
to gray and patches of white. I've seen each
lope to the table on the half-arm like a flat-
tired jalopy that has gasped away its engine.
I've watched them offer all their will
to sight, voice, and half their weight
in trade to the charity of memory,
if once more they could stroke a son's ballgame hair
or cup a daughter's wedding cheek.
I've seen hope's dream awaken
what, on the face of it, might seem
the heart's need to make amends,
to live out the rest of my mind's days
until I grow old enough to be young again.

Dropping Fuel Over the Pacific

Let the engine's loss of vowels begin.
Grind the tooth's blade, now the mind's
thin worm of denial through an ear phone.
When the attendant speaks, sweep the lone
bone from the dinner plate and weep.
The last meal is light. The silk
the child down-wind weaves in breath is worn.
Weep for the imagination's useless fire,
how the moment's fact loses what is prior,
and for the coiling smoke along the wings,
feed it water. The rotor, sleek as the Rolls
a dream could ride in, has coughed its soul
into your breathing, stuttering, losing weight.
Death will visit you in a foreign state.

Death Longs for Its Own Garden

where it can lean, tooth-picking, against a rusted pole,
where it can seem, all at once, the rose and the thorn,
the rope and the branch, a rotting tomato sac,
where it can heap the lucent glazing of an all-night hoar.
Death longs to sod the soil without warning what's beneath,
where it can bleed the stems of the ground's dicentra
into anguished leaves like unities of the mind's division.

It longs for the pick and dibble, the hose and shed,
where it can lie in sleep, nose-snoring flies above a skull,
where it can lay the mallow's nest in dried dove wings
or store the moon's shadow, the sun's ray,
breeding future in a seed, the past in a mandrake.
It wants to bleed the endangered prey of centuries
like a memory without witness, or shame.

Death longs to grow without limits, without rain.
It wants to gloat on the corpse of a planet,
segregating space, the dark from light
into colonies like crystal chips of frost.
It wants to curse the galaxy, its star-stubborn nights.
Death is a tired soul, gravely ill, spading a garden
for any discovery of gain, any recovery of will.

III.
Primal

We know separation so well
because we've tasted the union.

Rumi

The Penguin Stone

a

When a penguin calls to mate on the Arctic cap
and the ice floe tilts to tame his Chaplin waddle,
and where with stones cripped like bones in his beak,
he rakes the snow in tones as slick as a burble,
he will not stop until he drops
the gift of rocks before his heart's intended.
She, at first, is startled by the fool's panache
and glibly stares to see what scores of males will do
to match the offer. But stones are scarce,
and males still driven by a bone economy,
cannot afford rejection, knowing
how the female, if she's bored,
will swing her flipper to his noddle.

b

The wait is long and cruel as a rosary,
and though she drops her beak to nod
his broad bruised wing across her shoulder,
he will later find the gesture empty,
as dutied as the nest he burrows when the eggs are laid,
and where for months alone he bridles the brood.
She, away, will forage fish for the social order,
and climbing the land's high end, aloof and entrepreneurial,
will collect the rocks of fortune that she coddles,
and as she does, each penguin in the neighborhood,
knowing nothing lost is what is gained,
drops a stone to her feet if only for the privilege of her fervor
and the favor of a flipper to the noddle.

Primal

The leafings of birch unhinge in autumn.
The sod is maternal, a welcoming ground.
What isn't desired flocks to its own
for the soft pull of an embrace.

Should I raise my vagrant mind
to walk it sobering about
to find some lost relation?

Daylight has no memory of the night's
effusion, the stars it chooses to erase.
Winter has no nest for the sun's
breeding, the lynx no taste
to court the snowshoe hare,
my mind, no praise for the genius
in the hawk-moth's skull, conspiring nearby.

It's my daily rite
of belief's suspension,
to live each day for revival

in the diorama of April, for the renewed
grazing on a singular hope,
to breed some permanence of joy
into the infinite dimension of a grand surprise.

It's my daily leap
into the mind's
ennui, through the dizziness

of doubt unwilling
to restore the lost inspiration to a song
or a symphony's creation. I leap
to free invention, past the ignorance,
past the ignominy in all acts forgiven
or the repetition of a slap long forgotten.

By whatever means,
I settle on the will
to jump clear of the liar's kingdom

into the sovereignty of conscience
where a thought can breed
a bud of vision out of mediocrity
into a moment of genius. I begin by dancing,
over all objection, jumping

out of step
with the whole of my blindness,
until I see. I will be

like the cricket
that rubs its wings to create
a night's song of joyful stridulation.
I'll jump into the imagination
with a passion most will leap without.
I'll sing my anthem to the universe,

a warbler on a wire
with the will to fly. And with no
limits to my thoughts, I'll rise.

Taming the Sloth

I don't know how long I can play with a sloth,
how long I can wait to time his glide
along a space no wider than his bulbous face,
as if the air had softened long enough to slow
each arm's motion to an easy slide,
as if by committing each inch of leg
to a longer stroll, he'd be cool and jived,
just as we'd rehearsed for hours,
the slinky hitching up of knees
to gather up his fur like bunched underwear.
He's stalling now for the little push
my hand decides to get a rhythm going,
to quicken the pace, to push ahead
just enough to score the next ride.
How long can I stand the indifference
of his cold stare burrowed into mine,
as if he's judging a dance
where no one commits to lead or count in step.
I don't know how long he can lie
in one place, cheering his lack of progress.
Now, he's rolling round to his spine,
seeing the world from the bottom up,
believing this is knowledge of a kind,
having spent his clowning days
hanging downward by his toes,
trolling the uncertainties of ground,
as if by giving up a life of swinging free
across the long thin avenue of sky,
he could teach me need, the patience
to dream, how to slouch into the future
with the soft tongue-peddling of my breath
and a little push from behind.

The Beachcomber

I've seen this moon before, loitering
about the neighborhood, a hapless loafer,
indifferent to the shanty *favelas* or the day's
samba scent of the beach girl from Rio,
who feels the sun strain of lying back too long
and sighs. In a moment she will tease
her fawned hair from the sand, spread her tanned
legs warming down against the cool earth,
her one last thought of love like her ring
abandoned. Each day at dusk, the young boy's
binocular eyes drift to shade the sun's late glare.
The moon, staring back, floats free
of the night's spray of fog, and like the yacht,
listing dry dock on the bay's edge, guides its bow
to the shores of the sad boy's eyes, the light
just short of fading. The moon is a voyeur,
tugging a lost cloud through the sea's soft kelp,
scaling the trellised steps of the boathouse
where stars and compass intersect the young girl's
thighs, and a lone gull pecks as near as breasts allow.
The night whispers, closer, come. The moon
can only stare, the thought of touch out of reach,
and shunned, as if by a truant sun, sadly turns
and climbs the stairs like a groom abandoned.

Imagine now below the same moon, a palm
is swaying tall, muscular in its song
like a flamenco muse clicking air between the fingers
to a sudden stomp, each foot daring to kick one beat
into a pair. Down coast the Malaga lights
dance the beaches into one, the lamps' glare
like a necklace hanging stars along the breast
of the moon, pearled in halves above the bay.
Where the sand pools against the boat,
a ridge of water laps the bow in leaps
like a dog trained high to teeth a bone.

A girl, a sudden presence, stares out to where
Gibraltar steers the moon's glide into stone.
She bounds one way, now another,
as if some force, pulling her, were gamboling back.
There is no dog to leash, no mounds or rivulets,
no shells to necklace into Picasso beads.
What is it she seeks to find in the ballet of water?
What does she see in its translucence?
Is it the absence of stars in darkness
or the moon, breathing light into her reflection,
into the rhythm of waves, chanting
soft as wind riffling breath
into the fertile heart of the palm, dancing free?

Let's Say You Like Horses

It's not the waking
I come to, spooked, a winded stallion
in quiet breath and desperation
but the moon in halves with itself.

You come slowly
to the dream at dawn, a mare
looking down along the bed-rock
I've whittled in your stream.

You see a dancer. You don't blink
nor think it's only water
on the face of glass changing.
Now consider in the calm

of your reflection, a full moon is hung
like a bridle. Suddenly and at the moment
of waking, you turn to caress
that blind side of my mind
you love to call lust.

For the Nippers and Pippers

...for the disciples of greed.

You'll find them hiding discreetly on the take each night,
and no one knows
when or how they got here, gassed in the fast lane
of all things crawling
where the women lizard by in snake, eel, and white
seal stockings, sinuous
and as sensual as the worldly charm of a Gucci
hand-purse stripe.

And with their Lauren Polo and their Sax slacks
slicked to their tan-
dyed flesh, the men dance humpily along, shirts split
to the "V" of their navels.
An old gold pendulum hangs strategically
from their necks.
They carry the burden of their parts, loping like stud cats
through midnight streets.

When they're abroad and pipping, they find each other
with a burly kiss and hug,
seduced by the scents of their own bodies, while in a moment's
turn reduced to back-biting
like mongrel dogs or Polar bears in heat in Alaska.
When they sip martinis,
they tip forward to the weight of their one cocked finger,
stone-stiff, like the tea cup
sip of a strung-high hooker or a Wall Street broker.

They're tight as their pants in doling out a hand
to the hand-up vagrant
and talk of fixed skin like retreads on a Rolls or Beamer,
nipping and swooning
in designer jeans like a horde of crooning hyenas.
While diamonds they forever
sow in the back molars of their teeth drip from their mouths
in syllables of "ooohs" and "aahs,"
they're fashionably hip to the hop of their flip language.

All night they nip and they pip and their minds go Bally
to the swill
of a swizzle stick, while the world gone coke
and war torn-broke,
reels them in like the corner pimp they're courting
for the morning prayer
of a smoke and a pill or the speed of a thrill
they nose-up for
with the pippy friends they find so *chic* while snorting.

The Need for Visionaries

The first day the skunk bleeds through the nostril.
The toes fold in spite of themselves.
Its one stripe lights a landing strip for plows
and wheels spreading fur like flak.

Its perfume remains a passing fancy
for miles of miles and miles.

The next day its soft beard slacks in lather.
The cocoon of the mouth opens to bright lights,
and the tongue sprouts a mole's foot in dust.
The odor of sage soaks in the lime
chalk of its one blind eye.

The trucks are laying gravel
for miles of miles and miles.

By week's end one eyelash flits asleep
before a paver. It blinks when the road sweats
as if to say it's not old blood you see
but the death of vision, a sudden shock

of absence that breeds like dead lilacs swilling out
to sway your memory into a caress.

At a Loss

In the quiet moment of dumbness, when I find myself suddenly
at a loss for words,
and a breeze sweeps its wings, up and down, across my brow,
low and fast,
enough to stun the eyes, I imagine thoughts flying through
the mind like that,
begging to return in timeless waves, wanting to be seen.
It's best to study
the shift the weight of lost words might make, in stops and starts,
or the way
the choice of a first word is remembered always in parts
as in the reeling
back of a film that's lost its place. It's not scientific,
but every word
has its song, every syllable or letter rumps about in beats
against each other,
swallowing up the space between. In time, another beat,
another thought,
and soon the words will come as freely as the swivel-round
of bumper cars,
with driving speed. In time, your mind's talk will survive
the battering about.
It's not scientific, but laughter also helps to revive it.

Notes on My Two-Day Ph.D. Discuss Party

The *Canto* drips heavy off my lips,
a strain on the loss of spoons
in conversation, a quiver at the knees
where the committee sits, itching plates

of China, a point to be made on Pound—
these aging scholars in the grading stall,
proving oral delivery the test of stamina
for the mind, for the etymology

of sounds on the upper lip,
a concentration surviving each bite
of meat ball and shrimp. I sit
limp in body, at the knees, my plate

a pound of lead. I've prayed ahead
for strength to pass the test,
this long toss of the word *"Moloch!"*
across their skulls, each scowl

assured my brain is dead,
a foreign tongue to the men who rule
contra-diction, short of the mark.
Tomorrow, you'll address Swinburne.

The Poet Laureate and the Team Captain Christ

I've become
the poor
misunderstood Cain
in the Church of Abel.
When I walk past
any book or blackboard,
I carry walls
of chalk
on my shoulders.
I am my own burden.

When in groups
of two or more
I am adored,
an altar of muscle
to be genuflected to,
sublime hero,
maligned by my own
tongue's grace
and pectorals.

Beyond my inspired
stage, balding,
re-searching
truth's soft touch,
the epistemological
pat on the imagination's
rump; at best,
related by a cage,
I grow useless
beyond that useful age.

In a year when speaking
as I must
of the times
as rhyme demands,
of genocide and worse,
they would have me
in my dotage,
silent, writing
belated birthday verse,

icons to nostalgia.
to be ridiculed, mis-
anthropied,
ex-communicated
from the team Captain
Christ.

To the Immunologist Who Studied Bald Mice

for Miroslav Holub

On the day you died I held daffodil seeds
in my fist, and once unseen,
released the first two or three,
thrusting them North to the star
you had set all our bearings toward.
They grew as buds that fed the thirst
in dust, stones, reeds, the rambling dew
of leaves along the stems. The others
I tossed down low into the shallows,
for the stream to lift you up
to mirror the heavens with its flow.
On the day you died I finished
lines in a poem I thought you'd die for.
I had forgotten the image you translated
absence into, as if the bald mice
you fed, would grow their skins,
and the tongue's cloth, undressed and torn,
could warm your syllables
enough to survive the wind's barking.
On the day you died, I began living
again for the words you died in.

IV.
Astonishment

Poetry is the language in which
man explores his amazement.

CHRISTOPHER FRY

Swan-Upping on the Thames

...the annual swan count by the Royal Guard

The swans gather each Sunday like choir acolytes,
arching white beneath the stone locks of the bridge,
as if the barge passing with its Queen's crew of Markers
had drawn them in to ride its sifting waves,
or their wings' play against the willowed shade
had promised them a painter's paradise.
Perhaps, my eyes alone directed them here
for the comfort of clouds low along the skyscape,
seducing them to stake a fire in the dark.
Their flight now lights the heart of the river,
giving the sun its cue for lying down to seed the hills,
giving me the eye to stare across the wide grove of thistles
to count each swan with the Crown's mark of becoming
heir to the Royal flock. They swill their way
along the spires, reflected from the clock-tower walls.
And seeing their immortal glide rise and fall
like snow sweeping out the stains of autumn,
I watch their slow turn on the river
winding to where all vision fails, and knowing how
in my shoes' feeble lift of walking on ground,
one sole leathers thin without the other,
I would want to round the bend or scale a hill
to free my nature, how each step like a swan's flight
must dream a continent to hurdle,
not by force of habit, but force of will— to soar
as high as the black mute swan, freed from the reign
of all things distinguished into famed extinction.

The Bitters at Henley

They say the Angel Pub on the Bridge at Henley
is a sinner's site, whose centuried panes
of ancient views will bathe the heathen eye
in the healing waters of the river.
Above the sloping footboards, where the bar-
stool preachers sing their devilish *plav*
in Brixton drawl and Yorkshire brogue,
I drink religion, up-country, out of a Guinness pint.
The whisky laugh I save for the river stroll
squeals the long line of gulls away
like skiffs tied one to another along the wharf.
Down river, dark clouds punctuate
the sky's language, and swallows circle
like spaced indentations in the postcard
shot I take of St. Mary's steeple.
I believe I will never pass this way again
and pray beyond the promise made, that I will.
There's a pedigree of fame in this city
that shakes me to the bitter's core
of knowing what I can never be or will become.
Artists must have known this on their pass
down the cobbled path to the bridge and pub.
I stand at the stone buttress, transfixed
like a character in *It's A Wonderful Life*
to the yacht's bell announcing my departure.
There's nothing more satisfying
than the knowledge in the sinner's pint
I've put my mind to look forward to.

Buying a Print of Van Gogh's Irises

When you own this,
you will sleep in the color purple
and think it is the leaf of an iris
or a highway of membranes growing
out of an orchid's flowering stems.
When you own this,
you will taste the *fleur-de-lis*
in a wash of lavender
and think it is your blood
pumping the heart of a river
through the whole of your body.
When you own this,
you will hear the river raging
in the leaf of an iris
or the stem of an orchid
or in your mind's blood,
and begin to think the canvas
into perfumes of angelica
or a symphony you seed
in every last breath of your pores.
When you own this,
you own this, and need
nothing more.

The Weight of an Umbrella

Before its slick vinyl could wing its carapace
out above the body's width of shoulders,

before the tin ribs could arch to challenge the air
it had displaced in the sudden lift of sky,

before the knobbed handle could power-up
the palm's easy grip of manipulation

to deflect the assault of an Arctic wind
or the full force of a child's fisted sword,

it had been a thing of furniture, hanging
as adornment off the carved oak stair

or the hook of a hat tree-rack.
Before I could legislate the crowning of a cap

on the hard breathing of my balding scalp,
it had grown to be a thing of need

like a walking cane or a tent restraining
the elements of a cloud's quick temper.

It had never denied its role in knowing
what history of wind or sun it had rejected,

what weight in swallowed drops it had to pay
to save the ground from the deep soak of grime.

You would think it might find a greater need
than saving such a brainless head as mine.

In a Time of Terminological Inexactitude

... a phrase coined by Winston Churchill
when contesting a lie in Parliament.

a

Sometimes I read irrelevance into things. I swear, although swearing
gives a coarser edge
to what I mean, an unfortunate cutting down of light in clarity
as if I'd chipped
some glass. Let me say it this way then, because in saying it,
I can be remembered
for my obliquity, the circumlocution, if you will, in what I mean,
and not be nimbling about
with words that bully-grind cruel laughter into conversation.
To speak clearly
with relevance now requires law, some rule of effort that defines,
that steals the moment,
creates no less a possibility than genius. I can't imagine
genius, that is to say,
to know its presence, I mean its prescience, when I see it, personally,
even if it lit up ahead of me,
because to know anything at all with certainty is irrelevant.
I won't swear to it,
because I've sworn off meaning what I'm saying. In fact,
that's what I mean.
It's all irrelevant. What's important is that I write exactly
the words I mean to mean.
And you hear exactly what I don't mean, and swear to it— exactly.

Sharpening My Wit

In times of turpitude, I sharpen my wit to find clarity, and compose
with a pencil, slowly
so as not to frighten the words. A typewriter socks and punches,
grips the page
by its lapels and undercuts the paper's belly with its fist.
A screen,
computer gray, will make a sentence shriek when all at once it's here,
now there
and moved about where no one cares like an army brat
whose sense of place
time divides, displaced by rents of space too casually confined.
When I sit down to write,
I need convention, an instrument of taste that turns a word around,
dressing and undressing
truth in the mind's mirror, primping it with forethought, with grace,
as if for a night out.
I need invention, a pencil that loves, that breathes the paper and mind
as one,
that wants to dance, and looking sharp, will jump and spin
and strut a few lines.

Mapping the Universe

It's best to lie together, feet spread for hours along weeds of spurry,
heads cribbed, arm to arm, your eyes scanning the long fields of sky
to see the one last star flirt with moons among the heavens.
In time, you'll breathe the odor of lilacs far beyond the high
lift of gantries on the clapboard barn. You alone will hear
the runty knots of spruce keen humming in a chorus of leaves
that winds of summer have seen fit to admire. And when you wish
that you could glide in sleep's blue mist, forever, to keep from waking,
that you could hear the crickets lead a symphony of larks
as tuned by wind as by their singing, it is then that you will see
all things radiant in the rain of light, and with both eyes closed,
you'll walk the moon round until the halves of earth
spin their hemispheres into a single web of land, how for every star
that night repeats, you could map the universe, together,
to learn what ground to stand. You will not be kept from finding
space above each other's shoulder on which to lay your minds,
to know how far and high your thoughts could rise,
how long your eyes could toss a star, to what firmament
of your imagination you could leap to cross the sky.

The Astonishment of Light

You have been in time so bright a light
you've fathered from the longest hour of day.
And passionately your words' *tuneful turning we inherit.*

And where the Dublin fields of heath and thyme
allow the mind's tormentil root to shroud or fade,
you have been in time so bright, your light

has nurtured all the world's impermanence we hold inviolate.
And now your breath antiques a planet's motion, the way
that stars do, passionately, your words' *tuneful turning they inherit.*

Say to the Liffey River as it bends to find the prophet
moon, breathe still and be for the horizon the heart-scape
you have been, in time so bright a light

to know what hope on the altar's stone a poem creates
to spite injustice. Imagination, for the mind's sake, pray
the passion in the words your *tuneful turning we'll inherit.*

What garland, what soul's dominion, what innocent slight
or timeless truth had you known or promised life to pay?
You have been in time so bright a light
to know how gratefully your words' *tuneful turning we inherit.*

...a villanelle for Seamus Heaney,
after a line by Dylan Thomas
in Memoriam, Dublin, 8/13/13

At His Dying Moment Einstein Whispered…Now

I have surely lost it all, my mind,
my weight, my commerce of laughter,
now…
a simmering coal of brief emotion sears
my lung to keep the breath from leaving,
now…
the ash my body stores for spring
has coughed its phlegm to sour snow,
now…
the dark, invading space within my skull,
has caulked my eyes' creations,
now…
the song the wind had once conceived
with aching rhymes, has left me
now…
reciting moans of a single word I hear
passing into obscure…no, relativ—
*now…now…*wait.
No, wait!

Under the Under

I have stepped in and out of caution,
the hurried gait, the spring and skip
around the angling bark,
the leaping out
                    and over

the pricked-up nail, the brutal
sting and curse that follows.
I avoid the jagged rock,
the puddled floss of gravel,
                    caked by light

and the dried death-wing
of a swallow, its flight filled
with the fury of winds,
once sparring through space
                    to a song.

It's the daily dodge, the unknowing
of knowing what awaits.
I've tossed it over
in my mind, under the loose
                    spindle

I've heard in doubt, pulsing
under the mind's breath,
the brittle beat spanning
the life of a thought.
                    It's the doubt

I hear when silence
insists on droning on, blinking
under the mask of witness
to a false fact, or to the sun's
                    sweating out

what's clear and evidential
beyond its radiant light.
It's the bud of possibility,
the tossing up of all
                                        that's under

the mystery of wonder,
into a throb of revelation,
the millennial trust in every truth
that's been denied, of war, climate,
                                            extinction.

A Room on the Irish Coast

I've known this room in light.
Outside the shadows graze on sea holly.
At any moment the May sun will leap across
the field to steal a glint from beds of aster.
There is little time to fill the ceiling panes
with night or peel the darkness off the shades.
The thinking here is gold in hue.
Rays that flutter through the blinds,
sheer as scrims, are kaleidoscopic,
latticed down between the light outdoors
and the slats of books within. There is no black
or white into which the mind need go.
I would think the sun might want the curtain
nearer, and of a kind that shimmers,
to show how vast and infinite are the whims of color:
emerald, sienna, indigo. All day their palette
reflects the bold insurgence of the writer's soul.
I could leap into the flow of it, barreling like a thought
down the Cliffs of Moher or along the Aran shoals,
a phrase shifting here or there, a syllable revised
like dunes or waves in poetry or prose.
All day the night imagines how in passing
through the shade of only half the world,
the light has lost what essence of a soul
the room preserves, how the mind inspired,
with all its memory echoed, like these words,
might endure beyond their telling.

The Venus Star

At dawn when the hour's late
watch me carry the body home.
Watch me wonder why the Venus star
outlives the moon, how the paling light
my ashen eyes reject has cloned its morning
image like a stain to the kitchen floor.
And once my final pulse is taken,
a thousand cicadas in heat, watch
the difference each thought's breath
will make, and listen.

We will make the trip together.
Watch me falling to the bed and see.
I know the words lie, hidden,
hearing the day's conscience attack
my spilling tongue to make amends.
Should I warn the sleeper there to wake
the pieces of my breath still whispering
syllables through her lingerie? Should I
dare to lighten her mind's sad breathing?

Words are never what they want to be,
never the soft solicitations of believing
they ring like chimes beating to a lark's note.
Never the gale's rush of wind retuning
chandeliers, crystal rising to a pitch.
Even now, a word is re-imagining itself,
unhearing the rhythm that gave it life.

A door opens. The piano echoes a cat's
toe on a key. I stalk its tone as if to eavesdrop
on some hint of absolution her dream inspires.
I repeat the note, lock the peddle down
to nudge the light into her sleep,
until the tone wakes inside me,
and I am left to hear a euphony of sounds,
a poem out of breath, spinning to untongue
the language from its dark thinking.

A stillness calms her breathing.
I chase its inspiration like the cat
side-winding round the bed to watch her turn,
one eye, pillowed in the firmament of sleep.
The other, opening, swans a welcoming smile.
I recite the poem, its final image fashioned
like the morning star, rising to light the trust
we shared in all our night-remembered joys.
What words are meant to do, just watch and listen.

after William Stafford

Acknowledgments

Grateful acknowledgement is extended to the publications in which these poems originally appeared:

Columbia Poetry Review: "On Lines I'm Not Sure Are My Own"

Eclipse: "The Penguin Stone," "The Poet Laureate and the Team Captain Christ"

Epoch: "The Bells on the Tabla Fields"

Even the Daybreak: 35 Years of Salmon Poetry anthology: "A Room on the Irish Coast"

New Letters: "Sometimes a Fly," "On Nippers and Pippers"

North American Review: "Blinded by My Senses"

Poetry: "Dropping Fuel Over the Pacific"

Poetry Ireland Review: "The Weight of an Umbrella"

Pratik: "Mugwampery," "Remembering My Lai After Leaving the VA Hospital Healing Farm"

Prosopisia (India): "Swan Upping," "Buying a Print of Van Gogh's Irises"

Rattle: "Taming the Sloth," "The Bitters at Henley"

Rattapallax: "On the Train to Cambridge, Through Ely"

The Rattling Wall: "Lament for a Milltown Son," "Let's Say You Like Horses"

The Southern California Anthology: "After All"

Sheridan Edwards Review: "The Need for Visionaries"

Spillway: "Sharpening My Wit"

Voices International: "The Venus Star"

Wilshire Review: "To the Immunologist Who Studied Bald Mice"

JAMES RAGAN is an award-winning poet and playwright. Translated into 15 languages, with work appearing in 30 anthologies, he has authored 10 books of poetry including *In the Talking Hours, Womb-Weary, The Hunger Wall, Lusions, Selected Poetry, Too Long a Solitude, The World Shouldering I, To Sing Us Out of Silence, The Chanter's Reed,* and Yevgeny Yevtushenko's *Collected Poems* (co-editor). He has read for 7 heads of state and at the United Nations, Carnegie Hall, for CNN, PBS, NPR, and audiences in 34 nations, including China, Japan, England, France, Spain, Brazil, Ireland, and the Czech Republic, etc. In 1985, he was one of four poets from the West, including Seamus Heaney, Bob Dylan, and Robert Bly, invited to perform at the First International Poetry Festival in Moscow. Vaclav Havel has praised him as an "ambassador of the arts." Honors include 3 Fulbright Professorships, 2 Honorary Doctorates, the Emerson Poetry Prize, 9 Pushcart Prize nominations, a PSA Citation, and the Swan Foundation Humanitarian Award. Ragan's plays, *The Landlord* and *Commedia*, have been staged in the U.S, Moscow, Athens, Beijing and Prague. For 25 years he directed the Graduate Professional Writing Program at the University of Southern California and currently serves each summer for 26 years as Distinguished Visiting Professor of Poetry at Charles University in Prague. In 1996 *BUZZ Magazine* named Ragan one of the "100 Coolest People in Los Angeles: Those Who Make a Difference."

Photograph by Tera Vale Ragan

salmonpoetry

Cliffs of Moher, County Clare, Ireland

"Like the sea-run Steelhead salmon that thrashes upstream to its spawning ground, then instead of dying, returns to the sea—Salmon Poetry Press brings precious cargo to both Ireland and America in the poetry it publishes, then carries that select work to its readership against incalculable odds."

TESS GALLAGHER

The Salmon Bookshop & Literary Centre

Ennistymon, County Clare, Ireland

"Another wonderful Clare outlet."
The Irish Times, 35 Best Independent Bookshops